ROLLERCOASTER MOONS

ROLLERCOASTER MOONS

collected *conservative* and *informal* verse
—a book of many moods—

LELAND JAMES

FIRST EDITION

Little Red Tree Publishing, LLC,
Connecticut, USA — Cardiff, Wales, UK

Little Red Tree Publishing
Previous books by Leland James

Animal Land, An Allegorical Fable,

Longberry's Leap, Children's Book in Verse,

A Mice Christmas, Children's Book in Verse,

The Little Red Book of Word Play—with Perspicacious the Cat,
—an Introduction to Creative Writing for Children

The Craft of Traditional Poetry,
—an Introduction to Traditional Poetry and Creative Writing

Layout and Cover Design: Michael Linnard
Text in Minion Pro and Ariel.

First Edition, 2021, manufactured in USA
1 2 3 4 5 6 7 8 9 10 LSI 25 24 23 22 21

Leland James photograph, on page 97 and back cover, was taken by John Robert Williams and is reproduced here by kind permission.

Front cover designed by Michael J Linnard. Images of the moons are in the public domain.

Library of Congress Cataloging-in-Publication Data

James, Leland
Rollercoaster Moons / Leland James. -- 1st ed.
p. cm.
Includes index.
ISBN 978-1-935656-65-4 (pbk. : alk. paper)
I. Title.
PS3612.A58565S77 2021
811'.6--dc23

Little Red Tree Publishing LLC
Connecticut, USA — Cardiff, Wales, UK
www.littleredtree.com

Contents

For Anndy, again and again...

Preface

Note to Readers: *conservative* & *informal* poetry vs. the *free*

What exactly do I mean by *conservative* and *informal* verse (*verse*, once meaning a poetic line, now generally understood to be poetry itself) and how do these differ from *vers libre* or *free* verse? And why does this matter? Many in the face of the contemporary dominance of free verse have turned away from poetry, or have thrown out all contemporary poetry along with free verse. It is my intention to address this condition by suggesting an expansion of what are generally two categories of poetry (conservative and free verse) into three, differentiating *informal* verse and broadly aligning it with *conservative* verse vs. the *free*. Also, in fairness to readers, I am here letting you know what to expect. Perhaps you will then open the book with positive anticipation, or perhaps based on a pure preference for free verse put it aside.

First of all in this disentangling, we are fencing with a ghost, free verse. The term as applied by many contemporary poets, journals, and universities boils down to "anything goes." I recently encountered a poem about poetry, a *meta poem*, in a prominent journal that included this line: "This is poetry because I say it is." This to me smacks of Humpty Dumpty: "'When I use a word,' Humpty Dumpty said, in rather a scornful tone, 'it means just what I choose it to mean—neither more nor less.'" T.S. Eliot—ironically often miscounted among "free verse" poets—attempted to put the ghost to rest:

> "[T]he division between Conservative Verse and *vers libre* does not exist, for there is only good verse, bad verse, and chaos." —T.S. Eliot

But the ghost did not die, and we arrive at a great share of contemporary poetry (chaos) and the need for clarity. As you have probably guessed this book does not contain what is popularly known as free verse. But neither does it exclusively contain what most people rightly think of as conservative verse. This brings us to the disentangling of the three: conservative & informal verse vs. the free.

What is *conservative* verse? Many will answer it employs meter and often rhyme. Agreed. Though, already, there is room for disagreement, some having more or less strict definitions. For instance, *perfect rhyme vs. imperfect* or *slant rhyme* (curt*ain*/ repeat*ing*, long*er*/implo*re*, these from Poe's "The Raven") or rhyme at line endings vs. internal or no rhyme such as in *blank verse* (unrhymed, metered) famous in works of Milton and Shakespeare. The definition I develop may differ in degree from another's with whom I am in broad agreement. Such differences do not, I believe, interfere with my general conclusions.

Conservative verse has a prevailing standard meter or rhythm. There are many standard meters. For instance, most commonly, iambic, anapestic, trochaic: respectively ta-TUM, ta-ta-TUM, TUM-ta, each rhythm based on both syllable and accent or stress, each comprising a unit of sound, a poetic *foot*. Metrical poetry usually and beneficially in my view employs a limited amount of substitutions of other metric feet. What does "limited amount" mean? Not so many as to defeat a prevailing rhythm. The various applications of meter within conservative verse are endless: length of lines (how many feet), many or few substitutions, patterns and types of rhyming, to name only the most obvious.

Further important elements of conservative verse are that it respects its roots in poetry past, back to ancient Greece and Rome, and it is—in another time this would go without saying, no more—understandable. It has meaning or meanings, most often regarding universal themes, death, God, beauty, the human condition, immortality.... Finally, conservative verse employs the elements of all great literature, metaphor, imagery, distinctive diction ....

More than half of the poems in this book are by the above definition conservative.

Bringing focus to the above definition, here is an example of conservative verse from Emily Dickinson, written in the literary

"Ballad" form (common meter) developed from the oral traditional ballad. It is constructed of alternating lines of four and three iambic feet.

I measure every Grief I meet
With narrow, probing, eyes –
I wonder if It weighs like Mine –
Or has an Easier size.

Note the perfect rhyme (eyes/size) and the rhythm. The lines can be sung to the melody of "Amazing Grace," with which they share, like many hymns and folk songs a rhyming pattern of ABCB. The meaning of the lines is clear. The poem employs metaphor, imagery, and distinctive diction, and the theme is universal, timeless. Interestingly, Dickinson's poetry, published in the late 1800s, was considered highly innovative.

Here is a poem of mine that might be seen as conservative, while some might think otherwise.

Prayer

"I pray because I can't help myself.
It doesn't change God. It changes me."
— C.S. Lewis

God is the wind, if I were a kite.
God is a mountain, if I were the snow
becoming a stream—and God be the sea.

God is a stone, and I a dull blade.
God is a potter, and I the soft clay
pressing myself against his firm wheel.

This poem is constructed equally of two different, highly related, poetic feet (iambs and anapests). *Strictly* speaking, conservative verse has but one dominant meter. There is slant, not perfect, rhyme with no fixed rhyming pattern (*God* is an *exact* rhyme, blade/clay). Yet the poem has an equal number of metrical feet in each line, and the diction is firmly rooted in the poetic past, root if not branch. The meaning, I believe, is clear. It is replete with metaphor and image. So, conservative? There is, as I will contend and shortly illustrate, no bright line—where I will in due course argue there is a bright line between conservative & informal verse and the free. Yet I believe the delineation is worthwhile. It will become, as we proceed, important in appreciating informal verse and become critical in differentiating *both* the conservative and the informal from the free. So, is this poem conservative? You decide. As you consider the question, I will venture a guess: your ear and eye tell you this poem may not be strictly conservative but it is not in the camp of the *free*—suggesting the need for a third category.

Here is an example of a poem, another of mine, that I see as conservative. It is structurally a sonnet (iambic pentameter, rhyme scheme)—yet a purist might argue it is not conservative, the historical sonnet theme being *romantic* love.

Stream

Above the bend, the water deep and clear,
the current strong; seen from the Buckman Bridge,
ten minutes walk for me, my cabin near,
through pines down from a timeworn granite ridge

—a lofty mountain once, it's said, in time
gone by. I come to see and hear the stream,
this part that of the whole makes not a line:
a phrase, a word or two, in the river's scheme

of mounting water up ahead that this
small stream will join; and that behind, upstream,
flowing down, winding from a nascent hiss
to sing a hymnal line and brace *the dream*.

From this unsubstantial perch, this swaying bridge,
mirrored in the stream, the sun floats on the ridge.

Now, the more difficult question: How am I defining *informal verse*? It may be metrical and rhyming but with a broader permissible space, fewer metrical and rhyming limitations, less *strict* than conservative verse; or it may have an alternative structure and rhythm altogether. Importantly, it shares with conservative verse a respect for the poetic past and, in addition to a structure and rhythm or music, it has meaning(s) with often a universal theme. Finally, informal verse, also like conservative verse, employs the elements of great literature, imagery, metaphor, distinctive diction.... Consider the famous modern poem by Ezra Pound:

In a Station of the Metro

The apparition of these faces in the crowd:
Petals on a wet, black bough.

Close reading reveals an iambic meter. The first line has six feet, *hexameter*. The second line is three feet, *trimeter*, and has a very common trochaic substitution (PETals) in the opening foot. An unusual couplet, yet clearly metrical. Also, the poem is similar (but different number of syllables) to *haiku* poetry, dating back at least to Basho in the 1600s. Now consider the poem's meaning. Focus on the title and the word "apparition," then on the poem's imagery in the second line. The poem may be understood as an enigmatic view of the human (perhaps urban) condition, a universal theme. Finally, along with *image*, there are traditional elements of literature, *metaphor* and *alliteration*. Notwithstanding the conservative characteristics, the look and feel of the poem (its brevity, extreme variance in line lengths, and abruptness) jars when contrasted with typical conservative verse, strongly suggesting the informal. Conservative or informal? Here again, no bright line. Despite the ambiguity, actually in part because of it, the dividing line is worth considering (finding what is common as well as different) in order to appreciate informal verse as distinguished from the free.

A clear example of a modern, *informal* poet, as defined herein, is T.S. Eliot. He often wrote in nonstandard rhythms, that is to say other than standard meters, while including perfect metrical lines. He was clearly grounded in poetry past and universal themes reaching back to antiquity. Consider this line from "The Waste Land." It is, as are other lines in the poem, in perfect iambic pentameter.

The chair she sat in, like a burnished throne

In other places Eliot includes lines from popular songs of his time, having their own rhythms. Still other lines are quotes from antiquity, and there are phrases from ancient poetic works. Eliot does not *conform* to any standard meter, his lines are of varying lengths in no consistent pattern, and his rhymes follow no scheme. He creates rhythm, a music all his own, and writes with complete mastery of metaphor, imagery, diction.... His poetry is then by my definition (notwithstanding the conservative characteristics) beyond the conservative border, not conservative verse; yet far from being *free*. I venture your ear and eye—pause to consider—will tell you Eliot's poetry is *neither* conservative verse nor *free*, validating the need for a three-part taxonomy. Listen to and consider these lines from "The Love Song of J. Alfred Prufrock":

Let us go then, you and I,
When the evening is spread out against the sky
Like a patient etherized upon a table;
Let us go, through certain half-deserted streets,
The muttering retreats
Of restless nights in one-night cheap hotels
And sawdust restaurants with oyster-shells:
Streets that follow like a tedious argument
Of insidious intent ....

Now, consider these lines from arguably the most widely read modern poet; by my definition informal, clearly beyond the conservative border, yet far from floating *free*.

The sickness of one of my folks or of myself, or ill-doing or loss
    or lack of money, or depressions or exaltations,
Battles, the horrors of fratricidal war, the fever of doubtful news,
    the fitful events;
These come to me days and nights and go from me again,
But they are not the Me myself.

These lines, of course, are from "Song of Myself" by Walt Whitman. They are not conservative by the yardstick of standard meter. They have a contemporary look (long varied and unpatterned line lengths) and their own rhythm; yet, I would argue, deep roots in the poetic past, most notably the Bible. Compare to *Proverbs* and the *Psalms*.

Here is another informal poetry example from Walt Whitman. It employs—as does the Whitman example above—lists, a common technique in contemporary poetry. Whitman's source of inspiration for the list technique may have been Homer, but more likely was the Old Testament. Again, listen for echoes of *Proverbs* and the *Psalms*:

> I hear America singing, the varied carols I hear,
> Those of mechanics, each one singing his as it should be blithe and strong,
> The carpenter singing his as he measures his plank or beam,
> The mason singing his as he makes ready for work, or leaves off work ...

Walt Whitman's poetry, as defined here, is clearly informal. The lines are of wildly different lengths, with no metric pattern. Yet they have music and poetic roots. Conservative and informal verse spring from the same well. Whitman and Eliot move away from the border between conservative and informal verse but they do not break *free*.

We have now a complete delineation of informal verse. The elements of conservative verse may be employed but more loosely and often in atypical ways; yet informal verse may have an alternative rhythm or music, much as Jazz does not sound like Mozart but is recognizable as music. Additionally, informal verse employs the historical elements of great literature, structure, imagery, metaphor, distinct diction.... And informal verse has meaning(s), often regarding universal themes. The distinction between conservative and informal poetry is not one of time. It seems so only when using poetic paradigms of recent (centuries) history. Both conservative and informal verse have existed at least since ancient Greece. Both are long standing, and they are first cousins.

Let's expand our view of informal poetry with some lines from Wallace Stevens. Stevens wrote in a conservative, flexible blank verse, tetrameter and pentameter, as well as informal verse. Unlike many of his contemporaries who wrote in meter (Robert Frost) or rejected meter altogether (William Carlos Williams) or wrote in some alternative form of rhythm (T.S. Eliot, Marianne Moore), Stevens alternated between both conservative and informal verse and created striking pathways between the two. From the Wallace Stevens poem, "The Ordinary Women":

Then from their poverty they rose,
From dry catarrhs, and to guitars
They flitted
Through the palace walls....

Insinuations of desire,
Puissant speech, alike in each,
Cried quittance
To the wickless halls.

Here we have iambic tetrameter cloaked by a broken third line, which accentuates the women moving *through* walls, as one moves by imagination from the everyday to the world of the cinema, ("quittance," "wickless halls") the everyday behind to attend an entertainment. Note the rhyme (walls/halls). Something new? Hardly. Here, from *Hamlet*, Shakespeare rounds a bit of iambic pentameter dialogue with broken first and last lines. Guildenstern, Act 2, Scene 2:

But we both obey,
And here give up ourselves, in the full bent
To lay our service freely at your feet,
To be commanded.

Again, we are at the border between conservative and informal verse, and again you decide.

Consider these lines from "The Fox and the Goat," a playful fable by Marianne Moore, a celebrated modern poet, and by the definitions put forth here, a writer of informal verse:

Captain Fox was padding along sociably
When Master Goat whose horns none would care to oppose,
Though he could not see farther than the end of his nose;
Whereas the fox was practiced in chicanery.
Thirst led them to a well and they simultaneously
        Leaped in to look for water there.

No discernible standard meter, but a palpable alternative rhythm or music. Try reading the stanza by taking away the word "there" at the end of the stanza. It completes the music of the stanza, which without it fails to sing. There are both perfect and slant (quite clever) rhymes, and the narrative is understandable, making a wry universal point. Informal, yes. And nothing *new.* Compare "The Argument," by William Blake, late 1700s: no discernible meter, but rhythm, slant rhyme (path, death, heath), metaphor, imagery, and a universal theme:

> Once meek, and in a perilous path,
> The just man kept his course along
> The vale of death.
> Roses are planted where thorns grow,
> And on the barren heath
> Sing the honey bees.

Informal verse is *renewed* not *new*: Eliot, Whitman, Pound, Stevens, Moore ....

Now, another tack, let us see what conservative and informal verse *are not*. They are not free verse, which by contrast typically has no substantial structure (prose cut into lines) or music. Additionally, free verse is most often opaque or devoid of meaning(s), *ipso facto* addressing no universal themes. All this in direct opposition to *both* conservative and informal verse.

Poetry critic Adam Kirsh, frequent contributor to *The New Yorker* and *The New Republic*, in his book *The Modern Element, Essays On Contemporary Poetry* describes many contemporary free-verse poets in the following way:

> " ... taking delight in writing poems where the syntax of narration persists in the absence of meaning, the poet seems to be telling you a story about him or herself, but the story never makes sense."

Kirsh further elucidates, as it were, much of the contemporary free range:

> "This is not nonsense as a computer spewing out words is nonsense; it is, rather, an evasion of sense. Each phrase and line has a certain weight and atmosphere, though one might be hard put to say what it is. Yet there is something impressive about this kind of writing."

Underpinning much of such contemporary free verse is a nihilistic worldview. We return to my early observation that free verse in its current manifestation is in large part a part of the postmodern movement in art: *the rejection of all religious and moral principles, in the belief that life is meaningless.* Nihilism is of course fair game in the world of art and ideas, and nothing new—Nietzsche reaching back to "Dionysian Pessimism," and forward to the 1950s *Beat* End of the World poetry.... There is much here worthy of barbs. But, in fairness, the floridity of the romantic poets devolved into greeting-card poetry, and, ironically, formed a rationale for *the new*, which boosted postmodern free verse, now institutionalized (academia, many prestigious journals) and dominant; turning, I believe, the discerning general population away from poetry. This current dominance and turning away is a subject in itself, too large to be addressed here. (See *Missing Measures*, by Timothy Steele.) On a positive note, at least from my point of view, I have as a poet survived, thanks to brave new journals and book publishers with open minds. Not long ago I would have been totally shut out by the poetry power brokers of academia and endowment, as I a conservative and informal verse poet was for decades. I published my first poem, after writing poetry from the age of twelve, when I was in my early sixties.

Free verse proponents, my view, in general, mistake the opaque for the profound, the exclusive (in-group information and perceptions) for the intelligent, and despair for a kind of courage. Another distinction: free verse tends to be self absorbed. Everything is all about ME. Universal themes (love, life and death, beauty ...) are generally eschewed, viewed as passé, or meaningless along with everything else. A final common element often found in free verse is the elevation of the ordinary; say a Walmart front entrance suggested to be a work of art equal to Donatello's "Door of the Apostles."

Here is a final approach to defining conservative and informal verse and differentiating these from the free. Compare poetry by analogy to the art of painting. The classical, "conservative" school in my definitional scheme would be representational, a *realistic* representation is depicted. The "informal" school, extending my analogy, would be *impressionism*, a personal impression yet still representational. Whatever is depicted is still recognizable for what it is. A tree is still recognizable as a tree. Impressionists, my "informal," would include Monet, Renoir, van Gough, Picasso … and yes at times, Leonardo da Vinci. A notable thing about the impressionists is that they all could paint in the classical style and, as notable with Picasso, many of them did so extremely well. The impressionist artists might be compared to Eliot and Stevens in the world of poetry, differing from the strictly conservative but retaining deep roots in the past. Informal, not free. Art in my view welcomes innovation but not a hubristic separation from the past. Conservative and informal verse are in my view both art. Free verse in my view most often is not, just as a squiggle or a coffee splash or a urinal on a museum wall in my view is not.

At this point I am well aware that there will be those in general agreement with my analysis and definitional scheme, and those who vehemently are not. I wish both groups well and welcome open discussion of which we have had too little in the recent past.

A final word on what to expect in this book. You will find a poetry rollercoaster of life, as it has been for me and for most of us I believe. I write and invite you to read according to moods: Part 3 if in a lighter mood, Parts 1 & 2 for reflection (read preferably in order), Overture, Part 4, and the Coda a mix. Or read in order to what I have imagined as the rollercoaster found in many symphonies from which I take inspiration.

I thank you for reading.

Leland James, 2021
Lake Bellaire, Michigan

"The Owl and the Pussy-cat went to sea
In a beautiful pea-green boat ....

And hand in hand, on the edge of the sand,
They danced by the light of the moon,
The moon,
The moon,
They danced by the light of the moon."
—Edward Lear

"Everything in the universe has a rhythm, everything dances."
—Maya Angelou

Acknowledgement

I would like thank my wife of now forty-nine years, Anndy, who lives through the many moods of a poet at work, travels with me and helps with readings, and supports me in a million other ways, as many as a rollercoaster has moons. Also, thanks to Betty Carlton, who proofs all my work with a devilish keen eye. Finally, my thanks to the editor at Little Red Tree Publishing, Michael Linnard, who selected my poem as winner of the Little Red Tree Publishing International Poetry Prize ("Spirit Road" included in this collection) back in 2015. Since that time we have worked together on four children's books in verse and a book on the craft of traditional poetry for children. He is an editor in every best sense of that word, making valuable suggestions, providing careful construction, and wonderful covers.

And special thanks to readers of my poetry, a truly diverse group—*The London Magazine* to the *Taj Mahal Review* to *The American Cowboy*.... My poems have appeared in a half dozen countries, with a previous collection being published in India. Readers in the UK were among the first to find my work in their journals and for that I am eternally grateful. It is a matter of great satisfaction to me that this collection is being published in both the UK and the USA.

ROLLERCOASTER MOONS

Overture

A Quandary of Jugglers

—and of those who fiddle with villanelles

Why does the juggler toss plates in the air?
What is the meaning? Where is the *reason*?
What makes him dare? Why does he care?

What is the point of tableware in the air?
Fame? Jugglers names might be *Grecian.*
Why do jugglers toss plates in the air?

Gain? rich jugglers like unicorns are rare.
Plus juggling's passé, quite out of season.
What makes him dare? Why does he care!

What explains the dinner plates *up there*?
It boggles the brain. It's just not Cartesian!
Why do jugglers toss plates in the air?

What is the worth of a foal chasing the mare?
Why angles Pythagorean? pastries Parisian?
Why are blue sapphires more than just rare?
Why are freckles so fair on girls with red hair?

Why does the juggler toss plates in the air?
What makes him dare? Why does he care?

Rendering Ruins

A barn abandoned, left to drift alone,
wind torn and breached upon the reef of time;
fields, now dust, where summer wheat was sewn,
the wagons heaped with grain stood long in line

to fill the grange of this once mighty ship,
now but a shadow, listing, ghostly gray.
Raw winds and pelts of rain how cruelly whip
the wounded roof and soak the rotted hay

—the roof, an April green in days before,
a farmer's name upon it stitched in white.
This ark of kittens, bawling calves, no more.
A rat gnaws on a crib, the final rite.

Yet on this easel, raised by bardic hand,
forgotten barns, *forgotten not*, still stand.

Inside Apples

I utter apples, as only I (and you)
can do. A tree can grow an apple.
Pigs with apples know what to do.
But I (and you) can utter apples.

"Apples, apples, apples ..."
Red, sour green, yellow delicious,
Macintosh, Winesap, Spy,
Jonathans in pecks and bushels ....
Snow white inside,
"Apples!"

In wintertime I smell them,
apples in my mind.
I pluck one down.
I take a bite, I hear the crunch,
I all but chew.
All, merely murmuring
"Apples."

I marvel at the mystery,
this utterance of apples,
here inside of me
(and you).

Fathom Flight

Who but God can parse a chime of wrens,
the tilt and swirl?

Or read the hieroglyphics of the hawk
etched on the sun?

Who speaks the language
of the swallows
and the geese returning?
Who can sing their yearning?

-and who does not start
at the beat of raven wings at night?

"Bronco Buster"

—Sculpture, bronze, Frederic Remington
61 × 39.4 × 17.8 cm (24 × 15 1/2 × 7 in.)
The Art Institute of Chicago

Lost rein
handful of mane,
one stirrup gone,
hanging on
forever
why.

Kentucky Mourn

This horse,
this explosion
of muscle
and primitive brain,

this horse, Intrepid,
laurelled, at stud,
walks—does he ever walk?—
dances, prances, struts
by the empty stall

where Ozymandias, his sire,
smooth-mouthed
these many years
has died;

once, like Intrepid
—laurelled, at stud—
Ozymandias danced,
his legs now turned to stone.

Frogs

in camouflage, sing armies
hallelujah-chorus dream
of turning into princes

I Am Jack the Cat

I am Jack the cat.
What could be better than that?
I am the most intrepid orange.
My claws are the spears of Achilles.
I purr "Fuer Elise."
I dance James Brown.
I nap Chopin by the fire.
I am Jack the Cat.
What could be better than that?

Fig Leaves

—after T.S. Eliot

Omnia vanitas

In our doing and undoing, in our designs,
the nakedness we try to hide,
the corpse beneath the sheet
laid out upon a stainless table.
Plainly there, plainly.
But we go on
in our intricate designs.

Panem et circenses

The clink of glasses, swirl of opulence,
a porcelain plate, the tasteful tie and jacket,
understated, elegant. Oh yes.
The anesthetizing doctor saying,
"Well at least he felt no pain,
or very little."

A fronte praecipitium a tergo lupi

And in a minute turning round,
the hours come and go
to find us old and disillusioned,
still longing for the clink of glasses.
Wanting more.

Or if we dare—
oh if we dare
to set aside our wantonness,
to cede the corpse upon the table
and hear, once more,
the voice that sent us scurrying
to hide our nakedness,
might these plumes of dissipation
in surrender

fall away?

Another Art

—a lover's quarrel with Elizabeth Bishop

The art of finding binds in weaves of rhyme:
the warp and weft of found and lost, and *after.*
An art to master, joining the threads of time.

A loom of beating lines, the past intwined,
lost days among the threads; a presence ever.
The art of finding haunts in weaves of rhyme.

A requiem of walks in autumn rain,
the stillness of the hills in misting color.
An art to master, bridging the rifts of time.

Find now a pungent sprig of fresh cut thyme,
the scent of love made long ago in heather.
The art of finding weds in weaves of rhyme.

And to the star of bitter Persian lime
add the perilous bloom of oleander.
An art to master, daring the rifts of time.

Go! *Find* again in lines of fair design,
weaves new, intwined in lost forevers.
The art of finding binds in weaves of rhyme.
Another art, joining the threads of time.

* See "One Art," Elizabeth Bishop

Pier

Set firm in waters indigo and gray,
she is a promontory; into mystery a way,
an anchor firm, a compass true, end stop
upon the rim of ever-changing day:

abiding sound, steadfast upon her rhythmic
stays, a *seasoned* way, prelusion span,
wind swept; a way into the main, a toran
into a sea sown deep with atavistic

shifting rhymes: and there a maiden vessel sails,
makes fast her lines upon new tides, explores
the untried shore, high cliffs, seabirds, salt air,
the haunt of risen souls, a world reborn

—and waking from this childing gyre I hear
a carol from the shore, an echo of the pier.

First Movement: Dark Songs of Light

Clocks

This spinning wheel of day and night,
the tides, first frost, a lake of ice,
trees in bloom, the river full.
Clocks of death, *clocks* of life.

My heart relentless beating drum,
the woman cycle, dates in stone,
a lighthouse beam's recurrent arc
upon the sea, a metronome.

Expanding heaven's starlit face,
the starlight reaching back in space
to when this world of clocks was wound,
and in that lace of fire, what fate?

Mainsprings unwinding ever down,
imperfect rhymes in *timeless* runes?

In Things Large and Small

In the late fourth quarter, some time to go
—the clock from here is hard to see—
the Green Bay Packers are down by 3,
when an icy rain begins to fall.

A cell in the upper tier goes bonkers,
and no one hears the call—no
not that kind, *terribly small.*
Insurance, radiation come into play.

Cheers from the crowd, Packers score,
up by 4, might win after all;
but there's the game clock still running,
injuries, weather, an official's bad call ....

A wobbling kick in the teeth of the wind,
cold breaths held in the upper tier
—the bonkering cell a marching band—
and the odd-shaped ball bounces and spins.

A game of roulette, the wheel spinning `round,
a field of Mad Hatters, the rain and the wind.
Does Design govern in things so small?
A Frostian echo: *Does design govern at all?*

Five Dappled Things

A wreath of twigs
upon the ground;
five eggs, cream white,
flecked gray and brown.

An ark dislodged
—a callous jay,
a heartless wind—
the nest set down.

A slant of sun,
a weave of twigs;
a future vanishing
—five dappled things

upon the ground.

Abandoned Barn

Broad shoulders bent,
    like a ninety years-old man,
wind beaten, sunboiled, in a field of weeds,
sinking down upon a stone foundation,
empty window-eyed staring in upon itself
    asking how it came to this and why?

Garden Basin in Winter

Water clear
beneath a glaze of ice.
Passed away another year,
snow melting into lace.

A thaw groans on the lake,
an urn of ashes
yet to find its place.
Gray light, a stand of birches.

Robins soon—*soon* will they return?

Tracks in the Snow

They led away from the village,
fresh in the snow, uphill beyond
the mill pond where no one goes.
The way steep, the winter cold.

I wondered who in the village
would walk up there in winter
—wind off the lake, sub-zero—
to stand and breathe the cold?

And then, in a moment, I saw
—the tracks were my own.

snowy backed deer
in the gray maple wood
at first light

Once

garden shears
upon a low stone wall
where white roses grew

a toppled pedestal
the basin lying near
mouthful of rank water

an angelic stone child
stands still by the gate
keeping the watch

A Pantoum of Wager

God said to Satan: Have you seen my servant Job, a man who fears God and shuns evil. Satan replied: You've bought him with blessings. Take them away and he'll spit in your eye. God said to Satan: OK, I'll take that bet. He's yours. Have at him. We'll see.

—the story of Job, The Bible

A wager of God's shall we ponder
—threads baroque as spider's web,
an hourglass of supreme torture—
the serpentine suffering of Job!

Threads baroque as spider's web,
celestial grant of Satanic torment!
The serpentine suffering of Job!
Who fathoms the rune of Job's lament?

Celestial grant of Satanic torment!
"Who *is* this that *darkeneth* counsel …?"
Who fathoms the rune of Job's lament?
Where was Job when God made the land?

"Who is this that *darkeneth* counsel …?"
An hourglass of supreme torture!
Where was Job when God made the land?
A wager of God's, shall we ponder?

The Truth Hunters

Five o'clock, camp of the Truth hunters:
talk upon the evening air, round
and smooth as party balloons,
seeming almost casual, yes, within an amber egg of urgency.

Seasoned veterans all beneath the canopy,
canapés in hand, martinis, gin
of only the highest caliber,
arming to encounter the Countess and the Earl of Central Park

—such august company!—

Five o'clock, the hunting time is near:
talk of Truth, lightly as the hand
that lifts a canapé, eyed
critically before devouring, signaling the waiter to bring more.

Glasses, sweat-beaded, float nearby,
shadow monkeys overhead,
blood moon rising: talk,
well choreographed; beaters, less-favored, there to flush the prey

—an air of stalking—

Talk turns to *Truth*, almost casual, yes,
grasped like the beaded glass,
canapés in air
—as if Semele beholding Jupiter had never turned to ashes.

Ghost Riders

Wild horses on the moon,
great silver beasts
18 hands high,
hooves of steel,
breath white as snow—
Gone.

Wiped out
by rocket men
who never knew
—did not believe,
did not *imagine*—
they were there.

Rocket men,
whose forebears
rode silver horses
(on the covers
of slick magazines)
now haunt the silent moon.

Spirit Road

Above the 49th parallel:

The trace of an old wagon road
—like faded tracks in snow
or a man's passage through tall grass
an hour before—a phantom trail,
twists and turns through maple and beech,
around steep hills of pine, winding deep,
deep into the age-old wood,
the way of a wounded deer fleeing the pack
or a wisp of smoke from a dying fire.

Wild leeks in the air, the complaint of a crow,
the crackle and hum of a hornets' nest.
Winter's breath, faint as the smell of wild grapes,
yet there, always there in this high place
far north of paved roads and gathering places.

Small signs: the ghost of a wooden wheel
long baked in mud grown brittle,
a nail, a doll, naked, blind breasts, faceless,
a tree bent back, lodged behind another,
grown strange like a humpbacked man.
A dozen partridges, the color of brush,
completely without fear, move aside, disappear.

A clearing: trees felled, trimmed, stacked in rows.
An ax, the handle rotted to dust, the head red with rust,
lying where it fell, having let go slowly over the years,
falling from the stump where it was left embedded,
losing faith in the hands that would lift it
and finish the temple, hands that never returned.

The cry of a loon on a distant lake.
A yellow leaf falls lazily down,
riding complex currents of sun and wind;
the forest sighs, a nearly inaudible sigh
—north, a far place north, north of the 49th parallel,
where a thousand years is the blink of an eye.

What God in This Forest Dwells

Trees utter Him
in colors,
fallen leaves, wet
smell of spring
—the crash of limbs
entombed in ice,
torn by winter's weight,
a gun-shot snap
before the din
of broken limbs,
a sudden stillness
lifting from the forest floor.

Trees speak His name
in sodden moss,
in wind-bent branch,
bark of brail,
shade from sun,
shield from rain,
gnarled roots exposed
clutching the soil.
Trees speak.
They croon, they moan,
they shriek. What God
in this forest dwells?

Shadow Fish

Below the falls white furl,
a silvered shadow trout;
where water turns to silk,
a blade of hope and doubt.

Faint smell of elder bloom
piquant upon the air.
The sun an alter bread.
The trout, my silent prayer.

How like the empty cross,
the ghostlike silver trout
—a shadow hanging there—
a prayer, a hope, a *doubt.*

The silvered shadow trout,
a *blade* of hope and doubt.

Dark Songs of Light

Far points of light in zodiac's black veil,
lights that brawl the night, heroes that race
from Babylon to Rome.... Constellations,
bright brail of lights, ceiling *Sistine* of stars.
Hieroglyphs etched bold upon the sky.

What lies beneath this scrim of distant fire,
beneath the trace of fish, of ram and bear,
Lakota's hand at rest upon Orion,
stars of luck, of love, scorpion and swan....
Celestial lights birthed dying into ice

—abyss, black mare; or chariots of fire?

Second Movement: Living Water

Howl

The wolf things came like smoke drifting low to the ground.
"I am lost and alone seeking God," said the man. "Do not harm me."
This was in the time before the planting of seeds, before stone walls,
Before fish and birds and crawling things were given their names.
The wolf things laughed, for they were really demons,
neither wolves nor smoke.
The demons had heard the man crying out to God.
But there was no answer, for God had given Man the riddle of life.
And God left Man to solve the riddle and in the riddle there
were perilous things.
And God had given the demons free roam of the earth.
And God was to man a mystery.

The demons surrounded the man and ate him.
They consumed not just his flesh but his despair and longing.
These demons, which had been like smoke, now became flesh.
Their visage was that of the wolf, for that was how the man
had seen them,
Mirrors of his own despair and longing.
The wolves were neither like demons nor like men,
But like both, like demons and like men.
And they were filled with the man's despair.
And they were also filled with his longing for God.
And they drifted like smoke upon the earth.

A Barrenness of Light

—a benediction on childhood

As if the word barren had risen incarnate
—no, that's not right—
had risen, stillborn, dead,
risen from the Black Forest,
from its deep Germanic roots:

The tree, a great boreal giant,
seen close, close,
close enough to touch,
twelve times the height of the boy,
its rough bark dull and dry,
cold as ice, touched, like fire,
this late November,
still without snow,
without the comfort of snow.

The tree, its branches withered
reaching up, beseeching,
skeletal fingers outstretched,
reaching, reaching up
without motion, as if frozen,
frozen in a moment of unbounded loss:
high in its branches a cavernous space,
a mouth, an elongated *O*
—a soundless Munchian scream,
a shriek, into the onset of night.

The tree, alone, alone, utterly alone,
even as it stands amidst others behind,
others ghostlike beyond,
all alone, each alone reaching up,
beseeching an iron sky.

The boy, turning twelve, cannot imagine,
can no longer imagine, cannot remember
spring, cannot bring himself to *believe*
in spring, in rebirth, in life after death,
not even a season, not here, not now
alone in his loss in the darkening wood,
alone in the snowless cold,
alone in a landscape of Death,
the roots of the barren tree
a great underground Beast

reaching up, reaching up for the boy,
drawing him down, down,
down into the frozen earth,
into darkness forever and ever,
in saecula saeculorum, world,
dark world, without end.
Amen.

Hidden, woven deep
within this season of despair,
not known, not then,
not known to the boy,
was another prayer, a benediction
there within his surrender,
surrender complete
to barrenness and cold: Death
perfect, transcendent, alone.
No, that was not right.

No, not Death transcendent,
not the perfection of Death;
this could not be believed,
a single eternal season,
an interminable season
of ice and night. No, it must
be the *absence* of something.
No, not the absence,

the *opposite* of something,
an arc of completion,

and the boy imagined
or saw, or saw something
and imagined: *a hive of bees*
alive in the darkness,
alive in this crucible of winter,
a hive of bees
high in the branches of a distant tree,
the sound unmistakable,
bees in flight all around the hive
bathed in pale yellow light—

gone the moment perceived.

North Lake

The arctic night
crawls down upon the ice.
Last light a strip of gray,
amber where it touches the horizon:
a tired eye about to close.
Tired of barrenness and cold.
Snowshoe tracks faint from the dawn
I now retrace on groaning ice.
The Ancient Beast nightwind howls
rising up in gales of swirling snow.
Away too long, too long alone.

No light shines before me.
Dark cabin windows mock
my coming from the cold.
No trail of smoke, the sunrise fire
long turned to shivering ashes.
My refuge reclaimed,
like my tracks upon the snow.
The cabin door frail as lace.
Rime frost, the morning fog,
winter's breath, crept in between the logs,
drifts, a ghostly shroud, upon the floor.
A skim of ice where water spilled
lies near the stove; a careless act,
like this late coming from the cold.
The winter unforgiving.
With habits frozen deep,
I light the lamp, I bolt the door.

The amber eye has closed,
ending the world outside.
Windows black as midnight ice.
The Beast now screams
against the cabin walls,

claws digging at the rag-stuffed cracks.
The rags hard frozen, brittle.
The Beast, enraged, grasping for its prey.
The lamplight faint, a jagged glow,
stuttering as if the rattled windows
were its voice saying I must hurry,
hurry with the stove.
The iron heart of northern places.

I choose the precious wood,
placing it with care.
A sacred nest of twigs I lay below.
In trembling hand, the match ignites.
I watch the fire awhile,
still kneeling on the floor.
The split wood blackens slowly.
Wisps of flame, like phantoms,
dart and disappear.
I close the iron door, listen for the draft:
the fire's first steady breath,
the chimney warmed.
Listening for the promise
that the flames will grow,
praying deliverance
from barrenness and cold
—away too long, too long alone—
pray to deny the Beast my soul,
drifting into dreams of morning coals
glowing like cherries in the snow.

Time Travel

I chance upon a sylvan glade, an Orphic
scène: moon threads, a lace of nightkin shadows.
A trill of breeze awakes the guardian trees,
live oaks in gowns of moss, tall runes of pine.

I hear the soft slow sound of fairy rings,
up from the inner earth, the *sacred circle.*
Fireflies, a skulk of toads; the dead come forth,
up from their graves in pagan conjuration,

sung heroes, hags, and godling visitations.
I drink the midnight dew, a witches' brew.
Tree bark I read bard-blind, Achilles shield.
I muse upon a knot of oak, a tangled root.

I lie with Gaelic nymphs in ancient vales.
The hum of power lines a mile away.

freak warm wind, *chinook*,
scythe of spring, windrows of snow,
exposed earth startled

The Secret of Fire

the secret of fire—
not flame, not color, heat or light:
music in a bed of coals

Tiger with Lamb

An early work of the Artist

On a mountain top, something like a mountain, empyrean:
He, a term of convenience; a tilt of the head, an expression,
shifting feminine into masculine beauty and back,
an effortless, ever-changing progression; *She*
stretches out her hand which moves as if holding a brush
making delicate strokes, dipping into an unseen pallet,
and a world is composed: a tiger and lamb, sketched and colored,
come to life beside a swift-moving stream,
a stream of great depth and clarity,
the stream appearing as if from a single brush stroke,
the surrounding land filling in, a green plain surrounded by trees,
foreshadows of those at the foot of Mount Kenya,
mountains rising up in the background, rising into cerulean air,
sunlight streaming down into a mist rising from valleys beyond,
the valleys and hills shaping themselves, a world emerging
a world from the Artist's hand, a miraculous contagion
and primal words derive: *beauty, freedom,* and *danger.*

Arctic Lights

Season of night, Alaska, Scandinavia,
Siberia .... The sun, Aurora, hides her face.
Light, opalescent, swirls the midnight sky.
A psalmody of light, an exaltation:
King David dancing, Ezekiel's astral fire
above the maw, the open arctic grave.

Noontide: a momentary ache of blue,
a tranquility of light, ascendant blue,
a Bethlehem of blue, a Eucharist of light.
From darkness risen, tamarack and spruce
attend the celebration; suspended night.
Blue light, lifting the shroud, the color true.

Moments of grace invade this world of ice
—veracities of light against the night.

Poor Death

—*the* thespian *sentence*

I've heard him, far off,
like a morning bird's twitter,
heard the scrape of his foot
like a shovel in winter,
seen his masks of cold stone
—blood, bone and seraphim—
heard the breath of his scythe,
watched him play the physician:

always on stage, ever the foil,
knows his lines, bows to the Author,
enters on time, knows when to enjoin,
holds a coat, sharpens a razor,

pacing the stage, or crouched in a corner,
plays his ace, calls for the sexton
—makes us weep, makes us mourn.
But Death lives *not* beyond the curtain.

Death, poor Death, condemned to play,
to stay upon this little stage.

Tao

Irony & Ecstasy
like Scylla & Charybdis
whirlpools of dark and light
sailing through
        the jeweled waters of afternoon

        sailing through the pitch of night
between the deadly shores.

Reach

A tree in Jersey grows
between two walls of gray.
        Reaching for light.
                Tennis shoes,
        laces knotted,
        hanging there.

The Bell of Light Being

floats in air
shifting its shape
like the bonnet ray:

an island universe of moths,
bright spots, moon moths
—like the ray's bright mottles—
cling to the bell,

some folded in sleep,
some press lightly,
some press resolute
on the iron hull,

some dance phosphorescent
on the crown of the bell,

forming, reforming,
transforming the bell,

like the ray
in salt water,
the tilt and slow swirl,
turning and turning
in a widening gyre,

—a myriad of souls
upon the temple bell,
the focused, refocused,
refractory bell.

And the miracle,
the *miracle,*
the miracle of the bell:

its tongue still tolls
within its shifting shell.

Adams Mountain

I gather in from this high place,
Adams Mountain,
my shadow sprawled
on shivers of stone.

Dusk drifts down, a shroud
upon the rust brown earth below,
autumn colors fading,
chimneys sending smoke up from the valley,
like prayers rising.

I gather in.
I see myself as from a far-off orchard,
a serpent's view.
My shadow turns to jagged lines
upon rough stone.

I accuse myself and seek a new
beginning, waiting to see a star, the first,
always having a little of Bethlehem's
forgiving light.

Stream

Above the bend, the water deep and clear,
the current strong; seen from the Buckman Bridge,
ten minutes walk for me, my cabin near,
through pines down from a timeworn granite ridge

—a lofty mountain once, it's said, in time
gone by. I come to see and hear the stream,
this part that of the whole makes not a line:
a phrase, a word or two, in the river's scheme

of mounting water up ahead that this
small stream will join; and that behind, upstream,
flowing down, winding from a nascent hiss
to sing a hymnal line and brace *the dream*.

From this unsubstantial perch, this swaying bridge,
mirrored in the stream, the sun floats on the ridge.

Prayer

"I pray because I can't help myself.
It doesn't change God. It changes me."
—C.S. Lewis

God is the wind, if I were a kite.
God is a mountain, if I were the snow
becoming a stream—and God is the sea.

God is a stone, and I a dull blade.
God is a potter, and I the soft clay
pressing myself against his firm wheel.

Living Water

Pebbles smooth as time,
checkered, boldly lined,
like ancient hieroglyphs
tossed by unseen hands:

ripples rise upon a pool,
by unseen powers move,
as if the *Mind of God*
has touched the water:

quieting, the ruffled silk
becomes an opaque glass,
how silent dark and still,
how silent dark and still.

Third Movement: The "Muse"

The “Muse”

A sailboat, small, unvarnished wood,
her sails a swath of toy-store red
fastened by type-9 yo-yo string
to a tilting mast and a pencil of boom;
a sailboat, small, unvarnished wood,

atop a bookcase, moored abreast
an amphora vase wanting Greek wine,
sprouting a wilting bouquet instead,
a spray of yesterday’s anemone—
Sea breeze! The “Muse” coming about,

full sail departing the bookcase bay,
close to the wind alive in the lines,
craft aslant traversing the blue,
past the tin-can clatter of everyday.
The “Muse,” into the main, on *our* way.

The Dandelion

—*Roundupped*, turned out

Suburbia frowns upon her sunlit face:
"Out out thou upstart *weed!*" Poor Dandelion.
Like sister Cinderellas, Queen Anne's lace ....
A beauty cast aside, no bed to lie in.

Medicinal, nutritious: a balm on scrapes and sores,
on insect bites; the *grape* of dandy wines.
Yet scorned, like salesmen door-to-door and whores,
where lawns like poodles have highborn blood lines.

Poor poets, children *pick* Dame Dandelion,
give her, a gift, in grand springtime bouquets
—gathered from yards the likes of lofty Zion—
give her a royal place with fulsome praise.

Oh callous world, stay your trowels of doom.
In your heart make room, let dandelions bloom.

Butch the Mercurial Cat

The cat, a tabby gray,
his coat a watered silk,
long whiskers, yellow eyed.
Oh! how that cat loves milk.

A boy gives Butch his milk
inside a castoff pipe,
the pipe a whisker small
for Butch the milk to swipe.

Yet, thirsty tabby slides
into the narrow way,
a curling wisp of smoke,
a curlicue of gray.

Like brother Cheshire Cat,
Butch has his bag of tricks,
a little magic act
that he does just for kicks.

The boy lies on the ground;
into the pipe he spies.
                        Somehow!
Butch has turned around:
a pair of yellow eyes!

A float of tabby tail,
then into thinnest air,
without the slightest sound,
            Butch isn't there!

Those Little Garnishes at the Café Surreal

On a floatsum island
down the Caribbean
in a bongo-bongo
place *très epicurean*
in me coconut juice
and de tiger milk gin,
I spy de scareful wake
of de hammerhead fin.

"Shark!" I cry.
Dis bring a long dead eel
in pink bowtie,
de Café Surreal head waiter.

He say, "De shark no please de mon?
You want a litto umbrella?"

"No, no," I say, "What else you got?
Some litty bite less scare so?"

The long dead eel, he smile:
"I bring de twist o' slug?
de octopus?
de black water bug?
de 'gator?"

Qui Qui!
I pick de water bug.
It swim so fine
dare in da gin
and jungle wine.

De atmos*fear*, refined it be
(Oh! de spiceful garnishes)
at de Café Sur-real.

Girl

Love's frantic flight, a dappled bird
alights within the junipers peeking back
through feathered boughs, balanced there
upon a trembled branch.

Two Trees

Pine
and palm,
like Philemon
and Baucis,
side by side
entwined

Now Once Again

How many years ago, I've lost the count,
we lay beneath these trees at springtime's end,
the orchard left to tend itself, for then
the children came and seasons tumbled all
into a swirl of summer days. Too soon
the verdant years were swept away, and we
were left behind like these old apple trees.

Now once again we lie beneath the trees,
remembering splendid seasons gone before.
A winsome smell, the apple blossom scent,
and Time, the careful gardener, cast their spell:
might apples once again grace these old trees?
It happens now and then in orchards old;
long left to tend themselves by nature's hand.

Now once again—I utter not a word
of this, of springtime's blush upon the trees;
nor seal with dulcet praise our quondam days,
nor point to cirrus clouds as they float by,
but muse the lines upon a fallen leaf
and tossing it away I say, "Who knows,
old girl, there might be apples again this year."

Mist

I like the fog, the mist, "cat feet," and all that.
But that's not the real *thing*, what I mean:
I like the hidden but not quite, the promise
of *revealing*. Not Avalon or anything so grand,
regular stuff, a swale along the road, a ditch,
earth movers emerging like dinosaurs, ripples
beneath a bridge, boughs bent to silvered water,
fingers trailing ghostlike interlaced: a curtain parting,
a promise, another day, little mysteries everywhere.
Scaled not to saints or laureates but to truck drivers,
bird hunters, kids on their way to school. The first curtain,
the mist clearing, the sideways curtain pulling aside,
announcing the second curtain, the main one lifting up
on the story, the dance. The sometime, someday.
A Promise in the mist, not just another morning.
The brush of a leaf, a tickling, an itch to look within,
beyond, inside, not just around, expecting *something*,
as if every day is the birthday of the world.

To the Nines

Sleek as an otter, your curves, my breathless beauty nine.
Flirtatious, feminine, feline, glancing over your shoulder.
Sublime in rows, like the Rockettes of Rockefeller Center.
When paired, a queen to that numerical monarch the *ten*,
demure in your place in procession, walking a step behind.
Oft times a monarch yourself, an empress, a royal score.
Dressed to the nines on cloud nine, nine times out of ten,
you dare, you go for it, gaining the whole nine yards.
You frame the very day for workers to toil, nine-to-five.
Cats have nine lives, *possession* is nine-tenths of the law.
Best of all, keeping time, baby is born in month nine!
Oh beautiful *Nine*, a beauty in youth and at nine hundred,
nine thousand, a million, a billion and ninety-*nine*.

99999999999999

José Pelican

The Mexican pelican,
an airborne ballet,
          a flying *gazelle*,
drops like an anvil
into the azure sea.
Leaky tub-like he floats,
what a wonderful joke,
this cast iron boat of birds.

Poetics the Ginger Cat

—Ποιητική: 'poi-EIGH-tee-keigh'

By a caged fire I read—around me walls
of ancient lore, philosophy, myth and war,
Prometheus Bound, Medea, The Sack of Rome....
Flames captured cavort behind glass doors.

I pause, plying the sage, musing upon
a well-worn Mediterranean page. *Poetics*
appears before me, gamboling my little stage:
        I watch the cat play.

Flute and sinewed lyre, a smirk of teeth,
the lightness of cat feet in Titian wreath.
What grace, bold shoulder, savage art!
        I watch the cat play.

What dread symmetry! Hammer and golden chain.
Cat paws toss, tease and bat. I gasp. I laugh.
I smile. I shiver. I ply this heart and brain.
        I watch the cat play.

If Aristotle kept a cat, its name
would be Poetics—a gamboling ginger cat.
Fire and ice and catnip mice: *Poieighteekeigh.*
        I watch the cat play.

Mr. Bumbley's Bad Day

Mr. Bumbley went to the cupboard
—the shelves were bare.
He called for help to his wife
—she wasn't there.
He got out razor and comb
—he'd lost his hair.
He thought he'd rest for a bit
—but there was a bear in his chair!
Mr. Bumbley looked in the mirror
—he wasn't there.
For poor Mr. Bumbley, please say
a little prayer.

Prickly Stick

Extatosoma tiaratum
—the "Australian Walking Stick"

Prickly Stick went a-walkin'
one fine day.
Hey-ho, diddle-dum day.

Prickly Stick went a walkin'
and he walks this way:
Hey-stick, Ho-stick,
Diddle-dum day.
Hey-stick, Ho-stick,
Diddle-dum day.

If you see him a-comin'
jus'watch him sway:
Hey-ho, diddle-dum day.

Prickly stick went a-walkin'
and he walks this way:
Hey-stick, Ho-stick,
Diddle-dum day.
Hey-stick, Ho-stick,
Diddle-dum day.

The Three Little Pigs

—a story retold

There were three little pigs, one, two, three
—roly-poly and pink, as pink as could be—
porkers that *talked* just like you and me.
Building their houses these pigs were, all three.
Two built their houses of stuff that was free:

the first built with straw, the second with sticks,
the third, a smart little pig, built with bricks.
Along came a wolf with a bagful of tricks.
He blew down pig's houses and just for kicks
had this shtick that he did before getting his licks:

"Little pig, little pig, please let me come in."
Said the two little pigs, "I'll not let you in!
not by the hair on my chinny, chin, chin."
"I'll huff and I'll puff …." Then with a grin,
the wolf took a deep breath and *let himself in:*

he huffed and puffed and blew down the digs,
the digs, that is, of the two foolish pigs;
those hasty pig-houses of straw and of twigs.
Gone were the houses of the two little pigs.
The wolf ate the pigs, dancing two little jigs.

To the third pig's house, Mr. Wolf came
—a wise little pig destined for fame.
The wolf huffed and he puffed, just the same,
but this little pig put that big wolf to shame.
A house built of bricks spoiled the wolf's game,

The wolf climbed atop the third pig's house
—that wolf was a *pigheaded* old louse—
he slid down the chimney but got a hot douse
in a kettle aboil on the hearth in the house.
The third little pig ate the wolf with his spouse.

Happily, the third little pig lived in his house,
in a house made of bricks, snug as a mouse.

Love Letter to a Spoon

How fine thou art my silver spoon.
Your neck as graceful as a swan.
Your hips full as the harvest moon.
Thy manner gentle as a fawn.

Bright curls of finespun filigree
Doth frame *the sun*, thy radiant face.
How splendid to my touch are thee,
Desire fulfilled in your embrace.

My lips you kiss, a fervent press.
I swoon above love's rapt bouquet.
Again, again I bend to your caress
In rhymes sublime of bouillabaisse!

A Warm Spring Brain

There's a pea-size place
in the human brain
that measures hot and cold.

Temperature, it's said
(those who ought to know)
can make us kind, cranky, or bold.

Waiters get more tips
on summer days
—tips get slow at *two below.*

In springtime's glow,
love fills the air
and wedding gowns get sold.

I think therefore I am, but only by degrees.

Bluesy River

—sonnet riff

It was a bluesy sound
comin' in off the river,
a mournin', woman-gone
sound, a saxophone's quiver,

the midnight mist mojo
risin' up off the river,
Pearly Brown in the shadows,
walkin' down by the river,

'round about midnight
got them down-river blues,
those slidin' past midnight
moanin' Coltrane-soul blues

driftn' down Bluesy River,
that lonely ol' moonshine river.

Those Sneakin' Premonition Blues

I got those sneakin' premonition blues,
those she ain't home, it's midnight, blues.
I ain't heard, I ain't heard, I ain't heard no news.

I got those took-her-cat-to-meetin' sneakin' blues.
I got those wore-two-pair-a-stockin's sneakin' blues.
I can read, I can read, I can read the clues.

Why'd she go? I never lied, never broke no rule.
I never spied she would go, ought to be a rule.
Loved her more, told her so, than my favorite mule.

Why'd she leave me, why'd she grieve me, never did no harm.
Why'd she leave me here to grievin', never did no harm.
Why'd she leave me, guess she didn't like life on the farm.

The Pear Pit

I fell into a pear pit
upon a summer's day.
I fell into a pear pit
and whiled the time away.

How sad will be the hunter,
as sad as he can be,
finding not a pitted pear
but finding only me.

The Revenge of Miss Tilly Conflation

In the nickel of time, not a farthing too soon,
she basted the dastard, she lowered the boon.

She settled his trash, threw the bum to the frogs.
He was her man, but he'd gone to the hogs.

This little lady, Miss Tilly Conflation,
she piled a punch, breathed inflammation:

One fist of iron, the other of gold
—he was her man; now he's down in the cold.

Plato's Pumpkins

A patchwork quilt of pumpkins sown with gourds,
odd fellows green and yellow 'twixt-and-'tween
October's orbs of orange the overlords
of cowboy, tramp, and witch come Halloween.

The pumpkins, large and small, a fertile ground:
goose eggs and horns and hooters, fat and lean
—the perfect pumpkin nowhere to be found—
thin reeds, split shot, odd knobs, pink tangerines....

The Perfect Pumpkin's ghost within us calls.
It beckons us to scour the pumpkin patch.
We look for pumpkins round as basketballs,
but mind sublime and nature do not match.

Perfection haunts the pumpkin patch within
—wry Jack O' Lantern mocks us with his grin.

The Headless Horseman

Comes the headless horseman, riding, riding,
spurring his dark mount, thundering over a wooden bridge,
colliding (the poor devil) with a tree on a tricky curve—
Ouch! Unsafe. Worse than texting while driving,
flying blind, benighted, on All Hallows' Eve.

A Quirkery of Birds

"Scientists still don't know what's causing
flocks of birds to drop from the sky."
—Los Angeles Times

A thousand blackbirds from the sky.
    I don't know why?
Neither do *they*. Nearby and far.

Not guys and gals with microscopes,
    not pres or pope,
not movie stars, not me, not you.

No, not a clue! to this *game* show,
    fallin' birds, like black snow
—like the crows of Vince Van Gough.

Just when we thought we knew it all:
        Curveball!

Red winged blackbirds, by the way.
Blackbirds fallin' at the break of day.

Rollercoaster Moons

"You are eternity's hostage, a captive of time."
—Boris Pasternak

I tumble from modernity
—this ever-shifting stage

no longer seeking encores,
done with revolving doors,
with temporal intensity;
discontent with opulence, oranges
and green-winged cockatoos on idle mornings;
ill at ease with self-absorbed soliloquies;
surfeit with vaulted songs of myself
—tumbling down, a vagabond

out of time

I ride the rollercoaster moons

Fourth Movement: Gypsy Cab

Gypsy Cab

—a self portrait

My gypsy cab, a carriage old,
        time worn, the traces gray,
pulled by an aging mare I know,
        as others know their wives;

her dappled coat entrances while
        by lamplight we wait fares
in silence joined, sketchbook in hand,
        rag paper and soft pencil.

We take our fares down narrow streets,
        bring them along in sway,
to the rhythm of the mare's light feet;
        my musing mare and I,

down narrow streets, skirting bright lights,
        to many colored doors,
deliver them, and then by lamplight,
        pencil in hand, we keep them.

Aunt Reba

Her hair was thin as thread, chalk-white and spare.
She kept it best she could, and spent some extra
time that night preparing her evening charm;
her nails long unpainted ovals like light opal.

Aunt Reba's failing eyes were blue, gone pale,
a watered silk, the color of the shawl,
in graceful drape, she chose to wear that night.
She had a glass of wine, quite rare these days,

at our dinner lit by one long tapered candle.
After the coffee and red-velvet cake, the candle
extinguished with a breath so faint the flame
resisted an instant, brightening before expiring.

Then, the first time ever, she allowed the smoke
from the slender ivory taper to rise, a whisper;
delicate strings of pearl-gray entwined a moment
above the dying wick, the first time ever

in the more than forty of her ninety years
when I had sat with her at this dining table,
she did not wet her finger, lips and tongue,
and squeeze the wick between finger and thumb

—I still hear the sound, recall the faint perfume,
saving the candle to burn another day—
the wisp of smoke from the candle slowly rising.
The next day, Aunt Reba was gone.

Hall of Mirrors

"Sure the exhibitors love me; I'm a two bag man! By the time I'm through shooting up the villains, the audience has eaten two bags of popcorn each."
—Audie Murphy

Audie Murphy, the most decorated U.S. combat soldier of World War II, sits in a Hollywood screening room seeing himself on the silver screen, baby-faced, almost angelic, mowing down Germans, tossing grenades —he is playing himself in the movie version of his autobiography. This Audie, the one viewing *the other* on the screen, recalls in the pages of his autobiography, a third Audie clearing snipers from Montélimar, a French town known for elegant desserts, a town later celebrated by the Beatles: "Savoy Truffle": *Creme tangerine and Montélimar ....*

Audie recalls his own ghost-written self from his autobiography, seeing himself *over there* on the big screen, remembering the real thing: *"Leaping from the sunlight into the dim rooms, we must wait for our eyes to become adjusted.... Suddenly I find myself faced by a terrible-looking creature with a Tommy Gun. His face is black; his eyes are red and glaring. I give him a burst and see the flash of my own gun, which is followed by the sound of shattering glass. The horrible thing I had shot at was the reflection of my own smoke-blackened self in the mirror."*

(Near where Audie shot himself in the mirror, later in bio and film, this scene was reported by war correspondent, Eric Sevareid. A crowd watched while six French fascists tied to posts were executed by firing squad, shot multiple times with rifles, finished with a pistol bullet in the ear: *"Mothers with babies rushed forward to look at the bodies at close range and small boys ran from one to the other spitting upon the bodies."*)

The movie, *To Hell and Back*, was a huge success, a two-bagger all the way.

* Audie Leon Murphy, born June 20, 1925, son of poor Texas sharecroppers, rose to national fame as the most decorated U.S. combat soldier of World War II. He played himself in the movie version of his autobiography, *To Hell and Back*, setting box office records.

The Love Song of (Starbuck) Jones

And how should I presume?
—"The Love Song of J. Alfred Prufrock," T. S. Eliot

Harbored in an alcove of solitary space,
his heart a thrum of keyboard riffs, oh yes!
an image bold in text, his balding spot
redressed. Jonesy among the coffee beans:

his sequestered double-espresso soul
sending a salted caramel *Venti* kiss;
a candied butterfly in binate amber.
A digital coy Christian *and* bold Cyrano.

Magic lantern faces in theaters made of
glass; foregone the risk, the glint and grit
of oyster shells and beer, hands held along
a wordless waterfront—*not* (Starbuck) Jones!

Prufrock redux, unleashed, airborne, *assumed.*
(Starbuck): another love song in the ruins.

The Strange Cure of Silas Magoo

"The angel of death is abroad in the land,
only you can't hear the flutter of his wings."
—Winston Churchill, 1944

Swarms of unmanned buzz bombs,
each making the noise of a motorbike,
rocketed their way into London,
killing and maiming thousands.
The one overhead, near, *nearer,*
—just for you, my dear? —
would go eerily silent, then crash,
exploding with enough force
to bring down buildings, on average
thirty-eight people dead.
It was safer on some front lines.

Besides the carnage and destruction,
the psychological effect was
quite devastating. An entire city
was suffering from deadly
anticipation—the slow squeeze
of the trigger in a grand German game
of Russian Roulette.

Shooting buzz bombs down
from the ground was haphazard
sport. Ideas were afoot: harpoons
fired from tethered Zeppelins;
someone suggested giant
butterfly nets, and no one
laughed. A medium offered a curse ....

Silas Magoo watched from the top floor
of the Hanwell Pauper and Lunatic Asylum,
watched from behind a barred window,

bars that could keep him in but couldn't
keep buzz bombs out. The Asylum
had indeed taken some hits, but not
Magoo's wing. Magoo had tried butterfly nets
on his own personal buzz bombs, smaller bombs
but just as deadly. Flitting about
around his head. Killing him slowly.
His butterfly nets didn't work either.

German engineers fixed the buzz-bomb noses
with sharp cutting blades. The blades
cut right through the butterfly nets.
Silas Magoo could have told them
the nets wouldn't work. Magoo watched
and listened to the bombing, becoming
strangely calm. The bombs calmed him,
something no doctor had been able to do.
It seemed reassuring to him, being attacked
from outside by something real. He began to feel
quite normal. His personal buzz bombs
began exploding harmlessly in air.
Soon they were gone entirely.
The doctors assumed they had cured Magoo
of his anxieties. He was released.
Days later he was run over and killed
by a speeding ambulance rushing
to save the victims of a real buzz-bomb attack.

War, the human mind, German Roulette,
buzz bombs and butterfly nets, and
the strange cure of Silas Magoo
—no relation to the nearsighted cartoon.

The Lament of Whitehorse Billy

I never took no water with my whiskey.
I laughed at winter's busted pipes and trails
hip-deep with snow. I never bent; no willow
tree was I. Whittled sharp, like a hardwood stake,
I drove myself into this froze-up earth.
I mocked the winter's dark and stood my ground.

Hard and strong I loved my brown-eyed Anna.
She loved me back and we was like twin cormorants
that never left the lake in dead of winter.
Birds not fine or flyin' high but rugged
like the tundra. Proud a little, Anna and me,
of the way we held our own in this hard place;

the place that we, Anna and me, was born.
Then a woeful wind came whinin' down the mountain,
cut me like a Humbolt ax, dropped me to the ground.
My Anna upped and died. I shattered, slid,
like a sheet of ice lost its grip, slid from the roof
into a bed of gravel. The doc, he told me

why, some words I didn't understand.
I hardly even listened. Why don't matter.
Dead is dead. Anna was dead and *gone.*
I'm hopin' folks remember me the way
I was before—not like now, gone all to Hell,
drinkin' from the bottle, lettin' the stove run dry.

I'll be rememb'rin' Anna when I bring
my .45 way up in the hills, where I
won't be to no one any trouble. Someday
someone will find my gun lyin' all rusted
in the snow. Let it be my marker. I hope
whoever finds it knew us *when* and says

a little prayer, for me and for my Anna.

Stone Water Pass

Rock face staring down,
the mountain pondered
by faint winter light,
rivulets of freezing water

—a man alone, lost
his thirty-years wife—

layers of rock, stripes of ice,
a silence of stone,
and the road slipping away
back down the mountain.

Aftershocks

A row of chattered hens,
a smell like rotting fish
and lavender.
Mortician masks, one beside
the other in the coffin.
Raspberries and cream
on Sunday mornings,
lingering perfume
faint as apple scent in fall
—mad yellow gas
creeping beneath the door.
A doe's head
stuffed with daffodils
upon the wall.
The walls as soft as butter.
A calendar of needles,
days torn, bleeding on the floor.
No more.
And words words, a roar,
breaking like glass upon the shore.

At the Nursing Home

—an old man vacant by the window

Hold me occasionally for the light is fading
and I can no longer see the hills that once
rose there, brown hills, sand, sand. I see
the color, like the brown shoulders of a girl
I knew by the lake, outside the window.
Did I marry her? Were there children?
Is that snow? Is it winter already again?

I remember her shoulders, not her face
or name. I remember your face sometimes
(are they your shoulders?) and your touch.
Hold me occasionally. The hills are gone,
and monotony. I know that word, but I
could not say it and no longer even try.
A strange world, monopoly. It tastes like bleach.

My life is there in a thimble on the night stand
only I can see. I stare at it for hours. Hold me
occasionally. There is no hurry. The light fades
slowly. It seems the last part of some other day,
and the thimble holds so little. The hills are gone
and soon the thimble will tip slowly over.
It will make no sound, nothing will spill.

Calcutta

—a fevered night wandering

In the mirror of his vanity
Death surveys
an agony of souls:
foul-breathed old men,
spent women, children
strewn like cards upon the floor
wearing his face.

A solitary nun in black
and spotless white,
ghostlike floats within the mirror,
a royal flush upon her cheek,
whispering against all odds
God's love, His secret will
—her undying passion.

Soul woman:
a beacon in the deadly dark
night of the human heart
joyously singing.

Death, where is your victory?

Last Planet from the Sun

—the lament of an aging whore

I've lived on how many
planets now
bus rides away

was in a movie one time
that kind

worked in cheap motels (the kind
where you can smoke) swam
naked in those tiny pools

Ever dreamed you was
in a room ain't got no doors?

Now is come and gone
—last planet from the sun—
after ain't even
the day before no more

I missed a plane one time
funny I remember that
but can't remember *where*

I was going ....

Ever bought a puzzle
at a secondhand store?

Ain't no life on this planet
nomore where I've made my bed

in a room in a room
I'm leavin' soon from a room

ain't got no doors

Saddle Tramp

—like his saddle, hat, and spurs

Saddle Tramp, sculpture by Michael Garman.
Bronzetone finish. 21.5" x 16" x 10."
The Michael Garman Museum & Gallery, Colorado.

No silver on this cowboy's working saddle,
host to stray calves, bedrolls, and dry canteens,
carried beside lame mounts home to the stable,
baptized in thunderstorms and mountain streams
—horn scarred by years of lariat, grooved deep.

The cowboy's hat, a wrinkled map of sun,
sleet, snow, and rain—Montana, Idaho,
Old Mexico—wide rivers, seas of grass,
an open range. The hat his brand, his kind,
—the "saddle tramp," a "drifter," the "cowpoke."

Spurs: a whisper to his mare; to friends a greeting
—a silvery pair of melancholy timbrels.

Kaleidoscope Man

The old man made kaleidoscopes
from paper tubes and bits of glass,
gave them to kids, a neighborhood of us
who knew him.

The old man said to me, slightly drunk,
"It's how you see when you're old like me,
kaleidoscopically, not the pieces:
the *all together* differently"

—I nodded, understanding not a word of it.

The old man sorted among pebbles, shiny beads,
bits of glass, wood scraps and tubes of glue.
His workbench like his life I came to see
—shards of mirror everywhere.

"Not *once and for all*," he said,
fitting the bright colored glass and blades
of mirror, his fingers rhyming with his stories,
the all-together, lives before:

roustabout in circuses and fairs,
deckhand, cook, truck driver,
shoveler of dirt, manure, and snow,
a wife in her grave, far away.

(His daughter had taken him in,
but he didn't say much about that.)

The old man's fingers filled a long silence.
He was gone, then remembered me there.
He handed me the kaleidoscope: "The blue,
that's Montana sky, color of my Bessie's eyes.

"The red, that's Georgia clay, a touch a Colorado,
had a pard there, good ol' boy, name a Billy Joe,
could play harmonica and twirl a lasso—
and the black and gray, that's pourin' rain."

Mule Skinner

Granddad was a mule skinner, a *muleteer*,
though he'd have spit at such a word.
Mule skinners cussed—it was their fame.
And if you knew an ornery mule,
you'd maybe cuss some too.
Granddad cussed his share for sure,
at times at me when I was mulish,
or in his way. You didn't like granddad
but you knew he knew a thing or two:

Don't turn yer back,
get them hands out-a-yer
pockets, and when ole Caesar
kicks, and kick he will
—he's a mean ole son-of-a-bitch—
step in, don't back away.
Get close and he'll just push ya.
Step back and you'll remember
that day; same's true a-most
any blow. Exceptin' it's a
train: then say your prayers
and thank the Lord it was
a train that hit ya, not me.

You didn't like my granddad
but he knew a thing or two,
and you'd do best to listen.

The Temporary Man

He hadn't a last name, I had no first.
Gaylord was a "hired hand," I was "the boss's boy."

Gaylord was a drunk, everybody knew.
He'd disappear, now and then, for a day or two.
"Gaylord's on a bender," everyone would say.
Then, sober, he would reappear, a blackened eye
or knuckles bruised; but with a steady gait,
able at his work, the best among the crew.

When I was working high, higher than a boy
should be, Gaylord would find a nail to drive,
or mend with tar a shingle, within a yard
of me. If I was sometimes cut, pretending
not to be, Gaylord would fetch the kit
and, saying not a word, would tend to me.

He didn't smoke or joke, like all the other
men. No dirty talk, no brag or bristle;
no smile, no frown. Talk was there'd been a wreck
a long time back: he'd lost his wife and daughter.
Gaylord was a drunk, everybody knew
—but he was good to me, and best among the crew.

Sawgrass

I've heard of fighters out on their feet,
and guys on the deck knocked cold
dreaming they were up,
arguing about it after.

There are those who say
if a man knocks you down
and you can't get up,
bite his leg.
When you quit make sure
they put dirt on you.

I knew a *bum*; he called himself that.
Hated the *homeless* tag, would not wear it.
He'd work for a pint of gin.

Life had knocked him flat,
down for the count.
But mornings he combed his hair,
and there was still a look in his eye.
Not dreaming he was up.
Chewing on Life's leg.

"Melancholy Woman"

Pablo Picasso, oil on canvas, unframed ("100 × 69.2 cm")
1902-1903, from the Blue Period, The Detroit Museum of Art

the *whore*—

of those with syphilis
—the same of Pablo ached—
the prison Saint Lazare:

she would surely wither,
the ache in her unlocked,
unchecked left rotting;

Pablo's drape of blue
would fade, fall away
—her face a slash, a scar.

Not yet: firm, reposed,
this face Raimondi, Manet
knew well, portrayed.

And Pablo knew this face,
proud, eternal; recent,
his whore from Montmartre

—Pablo wrote
the artist & his model
turn your back
but stay in view …
(now look away,
anything else confuses) …
i separate day from night
and the starless sky
from the empty heart

the whore—

Pablo's whore of Saint Lazare,
with syphilis imprisoned
like others all the others

confined in prison cells;
the window behind *her*
rendered without bars.

Yesterday's Balloons

Balloon bouquet, red, yellow, green, and blue
caught in the wires electric. Like wilting flowers,
a few still vibrant tugging gently in the breeze.

An old man in linen jacket, hat; a street-side café:
he drinks vermouth, looks on a couple, eighty-odd,
hand in hand. She wears a brightly flowered dress,
he wears a bright red tie. The only dress and tie
for miles—the trill of ringtones in the air.

The old man at the table and the old couple, paired,
a Sunday brunch of daffodil and morning glories gone
among the denim hum and mobile portals everywhere.

Balloons caught in the wires, a birthday's lost bouquet
tangled in the moments surging on. The old man rises
from the table, doffs his hat; the waitress smiles
goodbye. She nods, never seeing the balloons,
their passing, not hearing the requiem of many colors.

Coda

Bend in the River

In looking back, it seems a moment since
the river ran, a fawn, leaping, cavorting,
and I beside like Ishmael down to the sea.

The river widened, running deep and fleet,
a playful fawn become a sturdy roe;
and I in its broad wake would reach the sea!

A bend, the river turning, rounding on
itself, slowed, moving into eddied pools,
echoes of the fleeting dream as evening falls

—my heart sung on the water like a leaf.

crickets owl
moonlight in the dock,
silver minnows laugh
                    tick-tock

Dusk

the acolyte of Night,
twin sister of Demeter,
winds down a spiral staircase,
yawning a blue-light shroud
upon the waning day;
a sacred rite of passing,
a silent prayer of shadow:
the promise of another season
written on the harvest moon.

Splitting Time

I split the wood each year
from rounds of beech and maple
bucked from the trees we clear,
those fallen from the winter.

Some say to split the rounds
still green and moist within,
while others find it good
to leave them for a time;

with these I am inclined
and leave the rounds to cure
beside the stacking shed
until the asters bloom

again up by the spring.
The rings within the core,
it seems to me with time
show faults that I may find

a truer line of splitting.
I leave the rounds to cure
awhile before I parse
the wood; my ax more sure.

Some say wood's split best green.
I'd sooner let it season.

A Song of Cedars

I am the singer,
singing of cedars
touching the sky,
but not the song
—the song—
written in me
before I was born,
the place where cedars
meet the sky.

Vanishing Point

My quiet craft parting still water;
ascent cradles the gliding prow.
Below, a prism world of shadows
in moonlight dart and disappear.

Familiar landmarks pass away;
the river widens toward the sea
—a metronome of parting water—
first light, horizon, curtain rising:

The sun, *an arc of fire*, bursts forth
—the steady sound of parting water—
the homeward ache of glistening prow,
the passing shore, the forest keep.

How can I keep from grieving.
How can I keep from singing.

The Moon is a Marshmallow

—where no one ever stubs their toes

On the Marshmallow Moon—

The Marshmallow Moon Mistress wears an old hat;
the king plays kazoo, and can't spell *Cartesian.*
Marshmallows are eaten all day, and no one gets fat.
No bedtimes or bee stings, broccoli or teasing.

The King and Moon Mistress can ask; they can't *tell*;
they play in the mud and leave buttons undone.
No one ever talks down, like kids don't hear well.
On the Marshmallow Moon, there is nothing but fun.

Ducks meow, fish howl; blueberries go moo.
People are green, frogs and grass are bright blue.
Don't tell science teachers, they'll say it's not true.
If you go there someday, say hello for me too.

Oh, I know, I know, the world is round not flat—
The moon is a "satellite object," astronomically,
and the moon is igneous rock, and there's iron in broccoli....
Never mind, on the Marshmallow Moon, it's not like that.

Previous Publishing Credits

The author wishes to acknowledge the editors of the following publications in which these poems appeared, some in different versions.

- "Abandoned Barn," *New Millennium Writers*, USA.
- "A Barrenness of Light," *What God in this Forest Dwells*, Cyberwit Publishing, India.
- "Adams Mountain," *Bethlehem Writers Roundtable*, USA.
- "Aftershocks," *Orbis*, UK.
- "*Another* Art," *The Lyric*, USA.
- "A Pantoum of Wager," *The Literary Nest*, USA.
- "A Quandary of Jugglers," *Form Quarterly*, USA.
- "A Song of Cedars," *Vallum New International Poetics*, Canada.
- "At the Nursing Home," *London Magazine*, UK.
- "Aunt Reba," *Inside Apples*, Moon Owls Press, USA.
- "A Quirkery of Birds," *Muse*, Collection, Kelsay Books, Aldrich Press, Collection, USA.
- "Arctic Lights," *Muse*, Collection, Kelsay Books, Aldrich Press, USA.
- "Bend in the River," *Muse*, Collection, Kelsay Books, Aldrich Press, USA.
- "Bluesy River," Literary Juice, USA.
- "Bronco Buster," *What God in this Forest Dwells*, Cyberwit Publishing, India.
- "Butch the Mercurial Cat," *Arc Poetry Magazine*, Canada.
- "Calcutta," *Harûah, Breath of Heaven*, USA.
- "Clocks," *The Society of Classical Poets Journal*, USA.
- "Dark Songs of Light," *Nomos Journal*, USA.

- "Dusk," *Inside Apples*, Collection, Moon Owls Press, USA.
- "Fathom Flight," *Vallum New International Poetics*, Canada.
- "Fig Leaves," *Vallum New International Poetics*, Canada.
- "Five Dappled Things," *Taj Mahal Review*, India.
- "freak warm wind," *Auckland Poetry*, New Zealand.
- "Frogs," *Cyclamens and Swords*, Israel.
- "Garden Basin in Winter," *Eyedrum Periodically*, USA.
- "Ghost Riders," *Vallum New International Poetics*, Canada.
- "Girl," *Osprey, Scotland's International Journal Of Literature*, UK.
- "Hall of Mirrors," *As You Were*, The Military Experience and the Arts, USA.
- "Howl," *Thirty First Bird Review*, USA.
- "Inside Apples," *Tipton Poetry Journal*, USA.
- "I Am Jack the Cat," *Allegro Poetry Magazine*, UK.
- "In Things Large and Small," *Common Ground Review*, USA.
- "José Pelican," *The Delinquent*, UK.
- "Kentucky Mourn," *The Road Less Traveled*, Dagda Publishing Anthology, USA.
- "Kaleidoscope Man," *Heart Poetry Magazine*, USA.
- "Last Planet From the Sun," *Gemini Magazine*, USA.
- "Living Water," *Taj Mahal Review*, India.
- "Love Letter to a Spoon," *Inside Apple*, Moon Owls Press, USA.
- "Melancholy Woman," *The Ekphrastic Review*, USA.
- "Mist," *Ruminate*, USA.
- "Mr. Bumbley's Bad Day," *Arc Poetry Magazine*, Canada.
- "North Lake," *Harlem Blues*, The Fish Publishing Anthology, Ireland.
- "Now Once Again," *Aquillrelle Poetry*, USA.
- "Once," *Reach Poetry*, UK.
- "Pear Pit," *CheerReader*, UK.
- "Plato's Pumpkins," *The Poetry Box*, UK.
- "Poetics the Ginger Cat," *Allegro Poetry Magazine*, UK.
- "Poor Death," *The Road Less Traveled*, Dagda Publishing Anthology, USA.
- "Prickly Stick," *The Society of Classical Poets*, USA.
- "Reach," *Magma Poetry*, UK.
- "Rendering Ruins," *Form Quarterly*, USA.
- "Sawgrass," *Evening Street Press*, USA.

- "Saddle Tramp," *American Cowboy Magazine*, USA.
- "Shadow Fish," *Blue Unicorn*,UK.
- "snowy backed deer," *Inside Apples*, Moon Owls Press, USA.
- "Spirit Road," *Paragram Spotlights Anthology*, UK.
- "Splitting Time," *Atlanta Review*, USA.
- "Stone Water Pass," *This is the Way the World Ends*, Finishing Line Press, USA.
- "Stream," *HQ Poetry Magazine*, The Haiku Quarterly, UK.
- "Tao," *Taj Mahal Review*, India.
- "The Bell of Light Being," *Nomos Journal*, USA.
- "The Dandelion," *The Literary Nest*, USA.
- "The Headless Horseman," *Thirteen Days of Halloween Anthology*, Local Gems Press, USA.
- "The Lament of Whitehorse Billy," *The South Carolina Review*, USA.
- "The Love Song of (Starbuck) Jones," *The Literary Nest*, USA.
- "The 'Muse,'" *Muse*, Collection, Kelsay Books, Aldrich Press, Collection, USA.
- "The Revenge of Miss Tilly Conflation," *The Eclectic Muse*, USA..
- "The Three Little Pigs," *Arc Poetry Magazine*, Canada.
- "The Truth Hunters," *Vallum Contemporary Poetry*, Canada.
- "The Secret of Fire," *Anderbo Prize Haiku Anthology*, USA.
- "The Temporary Man," *Cyclamens and Swords*, Israel.
- "Those Little Garnishes at the Café Surreal," *Barnwood International Poetry Magazine*, USA.
- "Those Sneakin' Premonition Blues," *Inside Apples*, Moon Owls Press, USA.
- "Tiger with Lamb," *Cyclamens and Swords*, Israel.
- "Time Travel," *Muse*, Kelsay Books, Aldrich Press , USA.
- "To the Nines," *Reach Poetry*, UK.
- "Tracks in the Snow," *What God in this Forest Dwells*, Cyberwit Publishing, India.
- "Two Trees," *Inside Apples*, Collection, Moon Owls Press, USA.
- "Yesterday's Balloons," *Carillon Magazine*, UK.
- "What God in this Forest Dwells," *What God in this Forest Dwells* Cyberwit Publishing, India.

INDEX

Poem titles are in bold and first lines in italic.

About the Author

Leland James

Leland is the author of six poetry collections, four children's books in verse, and a book on creative writing and poetry craft. He has published over 300 poems worldwide, including: *The Lyric, Rattle, London Magazine, The London Reader, The South Carolina Review, The Spoon River Poetry Review, New Millennium Writings, The American Poetry Review, Acumen, Carillon Magazine, The Dawntreader, The Haiku Quarterly, Taj Mahal Review, The Society of Classical Poets, The American Cowboy,* and *The Ekphrastic Review*. Leland was the winner of The Little Red Tree International Poetry Prize, the *Aesthetica* Creative Writing Award, the *Writer's Forum* Short Poem contest, the *Portland Pen* Poetry Contest, and was a winner of an *Atlanta Review* International Publication Prize. Runners-up have been awarded in the Sequestrum Editor's Reprint Awards, the Fish International Poetry Prize, the Welsh International Poetry Prize, and the *London Magazine* Poetry Contest. Honors have been awarded in the Bridport Prize, Morton Marr, *The Southwest Review*, and many others. Leland has been featured in *American*

Life in Poetry and was nominated for a Pushcart Prize. Leland's newest collection, *Rollercoaster Moons*, is published by Little Red Tree Publishing, both in the US and UK. www.lelandjamespoet.com & www.poetryfoundation.org/poets/leland-james

www.ingramcontent.com/pod-product-compliance
Lightning Source LLC
LaVergne TN
LVHW080310110826
845155LV00023B/110